THE *Archive Photographs* SERIES

AROUND MALVERN

Lewis's Hygienic Bakery in Church Street during the late nineteenth century. The shop is now occupied by Colston Bakeries.

THE
Archive Photographs
SERIES

AROUND MALVERN

Compiled by
Keith Smith

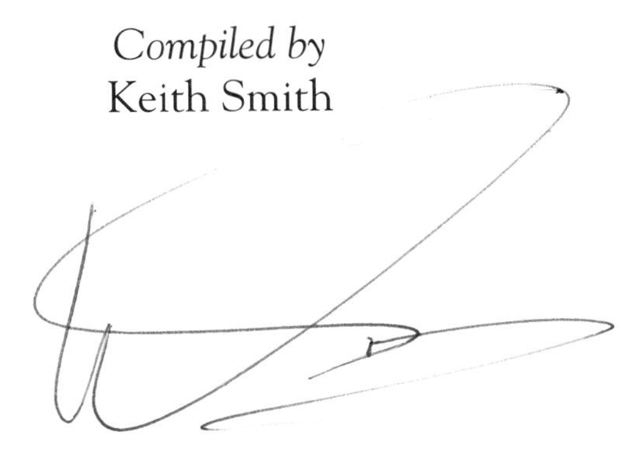

CHALFORD

First published 1995

The Chalford Publishing Company
St. Mary's Mill, Chalford, GL6 8NX

ISBN 0 7524 0029 0

Typesetting and origination by
The Chalford Publishing Company
Printed in Great Britain by
Redwood Books, Trowbridge

Contents

BURROW

Introduction

Malvern was described, in the nineteenth century, as the 'Switzerland of Britain'. As I write this, snow lies over the hills and throughout the district, and certainly gives an 'Alps-like' appearance to the area.

The Malvern Hills were formed over a lengthy geological period to form an impressive ridge running due north and south for eight miles dividing Worcestershire from Herefordshire. Both Midsummer Hill and Herefordshire Beacon were chosen by prehistoric tribes for encampments, the substantial remains of the latter attracting many visitors today.

Early Britons named the ridge of hills 'moel-bryn', the bare hill. In the eleventh century the name is recorded as 'Maelfern', and this has survived in its present form of Malvern.

During Medieval times the area was largely a forest, known as Malvern Chase, used by royalty and their favourites as a hunting preserve. Deforestation and enclosure occurred in the seventeenth century, after which much of the landscape we see today was formed. Enclosure continued at such a rate that the loss of common land led, in 1884, to the first Malvern Hills Act, setting up the Malvern Hills Conservators to protect the remaining common land. Today they control about 3000 acres of hill and common land.

Religion was extremely important in the Medieval period. Great Malvern Priory was established by the Benedictines around the late eleventh century. At the Reformation the Priory Church was brought by the parishioners for £20, but the only other part of the Priory still existing is the Abbey Gateway, which today houses the Museum. Malvern was unusual in having a second Benedictine Priory, at Little Malvern. Here again most of the monastic buildings have gone, but the eastern end of the monks' church is still used as a parish church.

In Medieval times, some of the surrounding villages and parishes were more important than Malvern. During the Saxon period Powick, for instance, was a vast parish embracing Newland, Madresfield, part of Bransford, and the Medieval parish of Great Malvern. As late as 1801, Malvern contained as few as 819 persons, Newland 132, and Little Malvern 34. Hanley Castle (which included Malvern Wells) had 968, Colwall 635, Powick 1172, Upton 1858, and Ledbury 3052!

Malvern was little more than a village, therefore, when in 1842 Doctors Wilson and Gully arrived and introduced the water cure. Local springs had long been famed for their healing properties. As early as 1756 a Dr Wall had testified to the purity of Malvern water. Even earlier, in 1622, water is recorded as having been been bottled at the Holy Well. The water cure, or hydropathy, attracted large numbers of well-to-do visitors including Charles Dickens, Florence Nightingale, Charles Darwin, Thomas Carlyle, and Alfred, Lord Tennyson. The water cure transformed Malvern into a fashionable spa town, but by the end of the century the treatment had lost most of its appeal.

Quarrying scarred much of the hills, particularly from the mid-nineteenth century onwards, and it was only fairly recently that quarrying ceased completely. The Conservators have done much to 'heal' the damage done, but the remains will continue to be with us as part of the Malvern landscape.

During the second half of the nineteenth century private education was a growth industry in the town, with almost as many schools as boarding houses catering for visitors. Both types of establishment are represented on the following pages.

More recently the Malvern Festival, started as a tribute to George Bernard Shaw in 1929, attracted many visitors to the area, and in 1942 scientists of the Telecommunications Research Establishment were installed in Malvern. Although initially resented, the scientists have eventually become part of the town and are now an essential economic factor in the success of modern Malvern.

The changes in shopping habits, coupled with the growth of commuting, have affected both Malvern and the surrounding villages. Many village shops have sadly closed, and Malvern itself has many former shops scattered through its streets now used for residential and other purposes

This 'potted' history sets the scene for this collection of photographs, covering a period of about 100 years. All the photographs are from my own collection, and copies can be obtained from

Keith Smith Books
32 Belle Vue Terrace
Malvern
Worcestershire
WR14 4PZ

One
Great Malvern

MALVERN c. 1860's from the Link Railway Station.

A FINE PANORAMIC VIEW of Victorian Great Malvern. The building on the left has disappeared to be eventually replaced by Lloyds Bank. The next two buildings formed the Belle Vue Hotel. Church Street is near right and is now much changed. However, surprisingly for a town centre, the majority of the buildings shown here remain.

BELLE VUE TERRACE and Worcester Road, about 1912. W.H. Smith is next door to the Metropolitan Bank, which is now Malvern Curtains. Both the Royal Library and Lewis & Son (on the right) are now banks.

THE VILLAGE PUMP! For a short time a pump existed at the end of Belle Vue Terrace. This view dates from the first few years of the century.

ANOTHER VIEW OF THE PUMP, dating from 1905. Why was it installed and why and when was it removed?

THE PRIVATE SMOKING ROOM of the Belle Vue Hotel, probably in the 1920's.

THE MOUNT PLEASANT HOTEL pictured just before the First World War, when it was run by Blackford Tipping. The building in the middle distance is the orangery, which has been restored in recent years.

THE MOUNT PLEASANT HOTEL, Belle Vue Terrace and the old Vicarage, taken from the grounds of Rose Bank during the 1920's.

THE REAR OF WORCESTER ROAD c. 1870's, showing the Foley Arms in the centre.

BELLE VUE 'PROMENADE' DURING THE 1860's. The gates on the extreme left are apparently the horse and carriage entrance to the Crown Hotel. The posters in the foreground are for auctions to be held by J.B. Harper and Bentley & Hill respectively. In this photograph

Belle Vue Terrace looks rather run down, in contrast to the usual impression given. The present Lloyds Bank was built on the site of the Crown Hotel in 1930.

ROSE BANK *c.* 1860's. The Wells Road is on the left. This avenue of trees has long since disappeared. About this time the house was occupied by Major General Wilmot.

ROSE BANK DURING THE 1920's. The Regency house was a gift to the town from Mr Dyson Perrins in 1918 and was demolished in 1959. Recently a proposal to convert part of the gardens into a car park was defeated by a local campaign.

PURSER & PEDLINGHAM, the butchers, were opposite the Foley Arms Hotel. H. Caldwell, the owner, also had a shop in Malvern Link and owned Cowleigh Park and Cross and Haffkey Farms. This view was taken about 1912. The shop is now much changed and has been split into a restaurant and travel agents.

JOHN ARCHER outside the Foley Arms, *c.* 1860's. At this time the Archer family owned the Abbey Hotel, the Mount Pleasant, the Foley Arms, and the adjoining wine shop.

RED LION BANK AROUND 1900. The single storey building on the left has now disappeared. The Temperance Hotel existed until at least the 1940's.

JOHN CRIDLAN, butchers, in Abbey Road, with the Abbey Gateway, *c.* 1870's. He appears to have taken over the business from Nathaniel J. Hemmings about this time. The shop has recently been converted to a restaurant, and the shop business has been moved to premises at the side.

THE PRIORY (ABBEY) GATEWAY AROUND THE 1860's. Note the stall on the right.

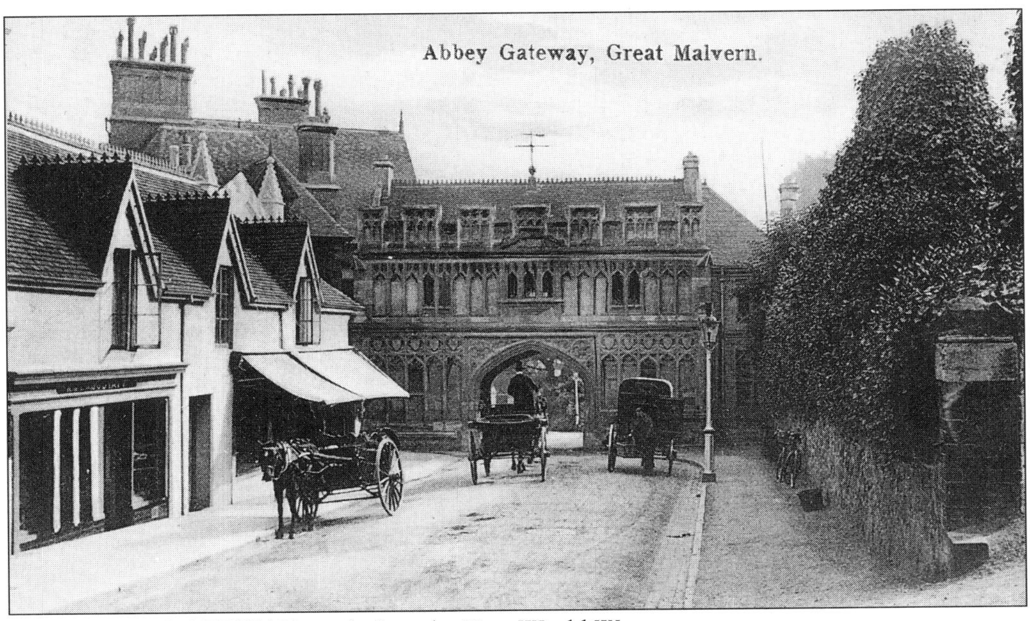

THE ABBEY GATEWAY just before the First World War.

THE PRIORY CHURCH, *c.* 1860's, from the Promenade Gardens. This view must have been taken prior to the building of part of the Abbey Hotel.

THE VICARAGE, ABBEY ROAD, IN 1856. The building was demolished in 1935 and is now the site of the main Post Office building.

THE VICARAGE IN 1867. Another view giving, as with the photograph of Belle Vue 'Promenade' on pages 16 and 17, a rather 'run down' impression.

PRIORY CHURCHYARD, *c.* 1860's. Note the stovepipe hat worn by the man on the left. The railings have disappeared, but their remains can be seen around the memorials. At this time it was described as North Hill Churchyard.

THE TOP OF CHURCH STREET about 1902.

CHURCH STREET around the time of the First World War. The Fermor Arms on the right is now the site of a shoe shop.

THE TOP OF CHURCH STREET during the 1920's. Vernon House, on the right, housed the India & China Tea Co., with the Blue Bird Tea Rooms over. The latter still exists, as does their hanging sign.

CHURCH STREET during the late 1920's. The shops on the left have been replaced.

GWYNN & SONS, established in 1852, were cabinet makers, upholsterers, funeral furnishers, etc., in Church Street, just opposite the Priory Churchyard. This view was taken around 1912. The business is now incorporated into Gordon Smith.

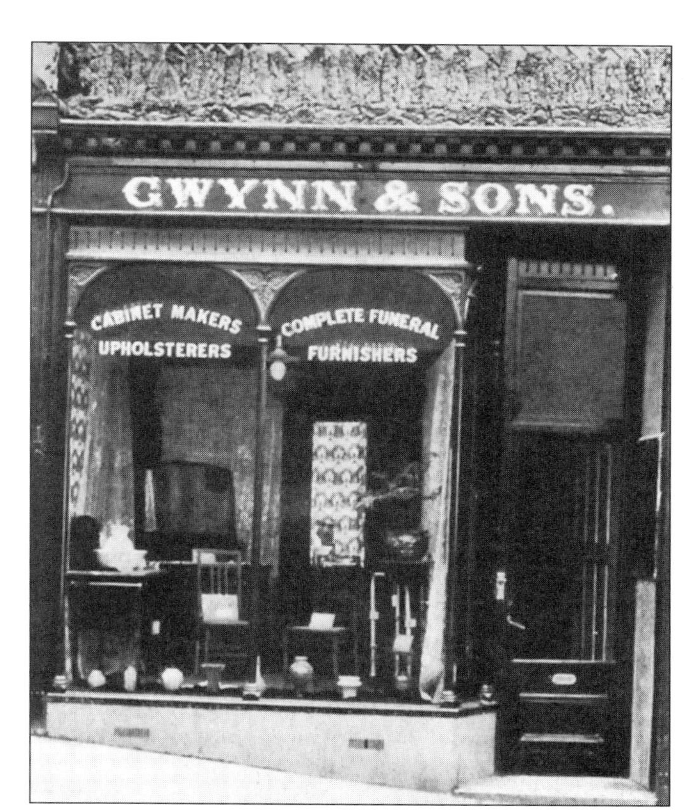

J.G. LEAR & SONS, estate agents, auctioneers, etc., in Church Street. This is the earliest known photograph of the business, probably taken sometime in the 1880's.

CHURCH STREET in the 1950's.

THE BEAUCHAMP HOTEL, 1951. The hotel, on the corner of Graham Road and Church Street, was built in 1843. A few years ago new owners changed its name to The Royal Malvern Hotel. Recently, 'Royal' was dropped from the title.

THE ASSEMBLY ROOMS were opened in 1885, shortly before this print was produced. The premises were extensively altered during 1927–28.

BEFORE THE SPLASH was built, the open air swimming baths were in Priory Park. This view was taken in the 1920's.

CLARENCE NURSERIES, Clarence Road, in 1906. Surprisingly, for a town centre site, these are still nurseries, now run by A.H. Potter & Son. The premises have little changed. The same cannot be said for wages – in 1906 experienced men were sent out for 3s. 6d. per day!

ALDWYN TOWER, on the road to St. Ann's Well, was a boarding house, run by Frederick J. Smith, when this photograph was taken in 1910. At present it is a nursing home.

MOWBRAY COLLEGIATE SCHOOL for girls, in Victoria Road, was started about 1908 by a Mrs Garner. It is now a much extended nursing home.

WELLINGTON HOUSE, Abbey Road, was the best known ladies' school in Malvern in the 1860's, when this rear view was taken. The school was started by Miss Jay, and is now split into flats.

MALVERNBURY, Abbey Road, was built in the early 1850's by Dr Edward Johnson, the hydropathic practitioner. His son, Dr Walter Johnson, assisted him and later ran the establishment on his own. This view from the rear dates from 1862.

ANOTHER VIEW OF MALVERNBURY, this time from the front, also dating from the 1860's. Florence Nightingale took the cure here on several occasions. The premises were rebuilt about 1907 and are now used as a nursing home.

ELLERSLIE in Abbey Road was built in the early 1850's and used by the Johnson's for the water cure. In 1936, when this was taken, it was a preparatory school and is now part of Malvern College.

ELLERSLIE was one of several schools with good sporting facilities.

THE IMPERIAL HOTEL and Great Malvern Railway Station during the 1860's. A very unusual view showing the station platform.

THE IMPERIAL HOTEL during the 1870's. Designed by E.W. Elmslie, it became Malvern Girls' College in 1919. When built in the early 1860's it was the only hotel lit with incandescent gas.

THIS PICTURE is described as a playground near Imperial (Hotel) and Christ Church. This would date it as around the late 1870's, but where was the playground, and to whom did it belong?

THE CONSERVATORY of the Imperial Hotel around 1905 would be considered rather overpowering today.

MALVERN COLLEGE SHOP!

MALVERN COLLEGE from the cricket field *c.* 1870's.

Two

Link Top, Malvern Link, and Barnard's Green

MALVERN LINK HOTEL and Railway Station 1863.

IN 1905, when this photograph was taken, this was known as 'Link Top, back of Worcester Road'. Now it is called Lygon Bank. The building on the right, Durham Cottage, was occupied by John Bishop, furniture remover. All the buildings to the left have now disappeared.

HOLY TRINITY CHURCH *c.* 1860's. The church was built in 1851 on land donated by Lady Emily Foley to serve the district beyond Link Top.

HOLY TRINITY PARISH HALL prior to the First World War. An imposing building which almost completely obscures the church from the Link Top side.

NEWTOWN ROAD, *c.* 1913. Bailey & Baker, grocers and licensed victuallers, is now Victoria Wine. To the right the corner building is now occupied by Teleradio.

GEORGE SMITH, confectioner, etc., at the Model Steam Bakery, Clermont, Newtown Road, taken about 1911. The building, which has not changed, is now the Colston Bakeries.

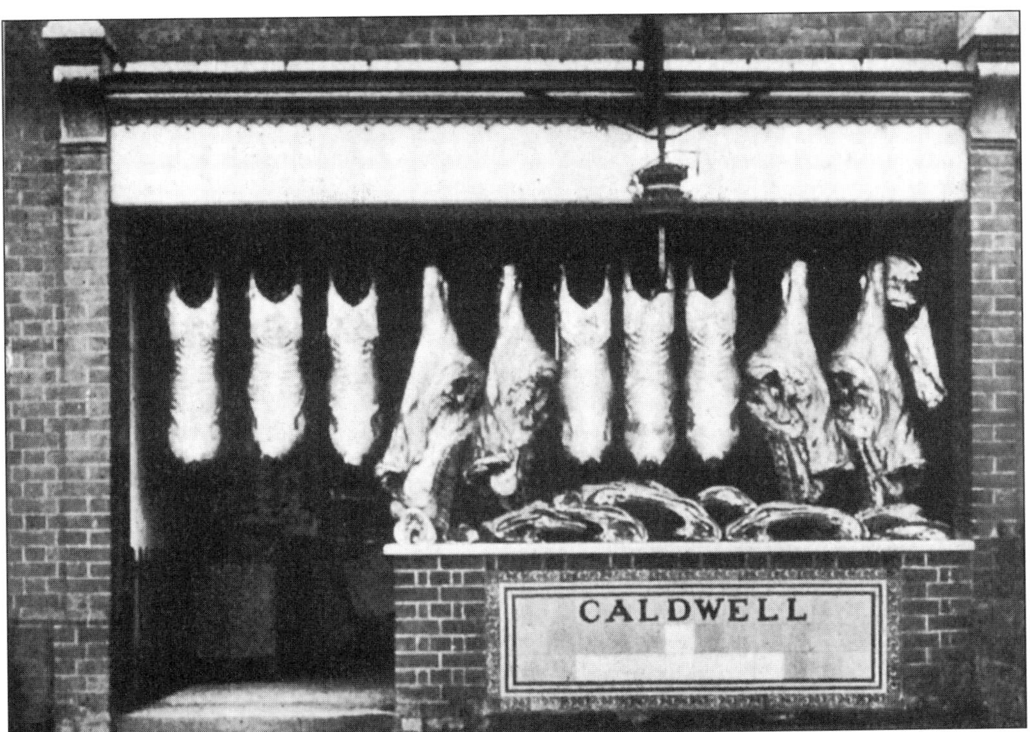

PURSER & PEDLINGHAM, butchers in Queens Road, Malvern Link, around 1912. The shop is now a bookmakers, but the hanging bracket is still there.

QUEENS ROAD IN 1907. At the time 'Blind George' Pullen, who played the harmonium at St. Ann's Well, lived in one of these houses.

NEWTOWN ROAD, *c.* 1920's. A. Wigley, on the right, was sub-postmaster, draper, etc., while Henry C. Hayes ran Newtown Furnishing Stores. On the corner of Queen Street, this is now Bealings.

ST. CUTHBERT'S BOYS' SCHOOL, Worcester Road, started by John Healey about 1904 and closed in the early 1940's. The house was demolished at the end of the 1970's.

SOMERS ROAD SCHOOL, Malvern Link, originally built as the Railway Hotel in 1861, converted to a school in 1873, and demolished in 1968. There was a fire in 1925 and this shows the school contents strewn over the ground.

MALVERN LINK CYCLE PARADE sometime in the 1920's. This view is taken on the Link Common opposite the end of Howsell Road. Flower & Sons, the brewers, used the store in the background from about 1918.

WORCESTER ROAD, Malvern Link. The Colston Buildings on the left were built in 1899. This view, taken prior to 1906, shows W.H. Rhodes, china and glass merchants. On the right-hand side can be seen S.L. Wade, restaurant and bakery, and John Hawkins, confectioner.

THE COLSTON BUILDINGS about the time of the First World War. The garden on the right is now the site of a discount store.

WORCESTER ROAD just below Malvern Link Station. Howsell Road is on the right and Pickersleigh Road on the right.

WORCESTER ROAD, Malvern Link, in the 1920's. The furthest house on the left has been replaced by a supermarket, and on the extreme right the trees have been replaced by a furniture store.

COTTAGES AT BARNARDS GREEN, from a late eighteenth- or early nineteenth-century painting.

COURT ROAD, BARNARDS GREEN, sometime in the 1920's. One of only two thatched cottages still remaining in the road. The building next door has now disappeared.

BARNARDS GREEN showing A.E. Baylis, dispensing chemists, and Williams & Co., bootmakers, just after the First World War. As can be seen, sales and extravagant claims are nothing new.

Three

North and West Malvern

WEST MALVERN from Cowleigh Farm before the First World War.

THE QUARRIES, North Malvern Road, with the clock tower in the middle distance, c. 1904.

NORTH MALVERN ROAD and clock tower c. 1919. The building beyond the tower has now disappeared.

THE WATER TANK, North Malvern, *c.* 1860's. It was built by local benefactor Charles Morris in 1835–36 to provide a water supply to the area. A clock tower was added in 1901.

THE WHIPPING POST AND STOCKS, North Malvern. The originals are now in the Malvern Museum.

THE CONVENT OF THE CROSS, Cowleigh Road, was run by the Lady Superior, Sister Calvary, when this was taken around 1916. The building has now been split into flats and is known as Cowleigh Court.

HOP PICKERS at North Malvern before the First World War. There were a number of hop growers in the area at this time.

J.C. WILSON'S Belmont Brick Works, off Bank (now Cowleigh Bank) Street, sometime in the 1920s. The houses in the distance are in Belmont Road.

WEST MALVERN from the Hills, *c.* 1919.

THE CROFT FARM, Croft Pitch, West Malvern, in 1921. The farm, which was owned by T. Jones, still exits.

ADELAIDE COTTAGE, just off the West Malvern Road, in 1911. The Darrell Brown family lived here between 1909 and 1917. It is now used as a Red Cross Residential Home.

WEST MALVERN AROUND 1925. The trees on the left have gone. The Broomhill Hotel is on the right, hidden behind the foliage.

MALVERN WELLS in the grip of winter, 16 January 1918. The buildings on the left have been replaced by the A.S. Daniels garage. The houses on the right are now a restaurant and Gandolfi House.

TOWNDROW & HOLBROOK, Post Office, grocers, etc., in the Wells Road in 1922. The adjoining building is the Malvern Wells Institute.

THE JUNCTION of Wells and Holywell Roads *c.* 1900. Compare the road on the left with the busy scene today. The low building on the left has been replaced by the Three Counties Garage.

BUILT IN 1843 at a cost of £400, the Holy Well has been restored in recent years. This view was taken in the 1870's. Water was first bottled here in 1622.

ROCK HOUSE, MALVERN WELLS, adjoining the Holy Well, around 1913. As early as the beginnings of the nineteenth century, it was used as accommodation for visitors to the Well.

MALVERN WELLS prior to the First World War. The fountain was erected in 1887. The shop on the right is Bedford House, which was occupied by Wm. Raymond Walker, a butcher.

THE GIRLS' FRIENDLY SOCIETY HOME, Hanley Terrace. Used by them for over forty years, it is now flats.

DINING ROOM of the Girls' Friendly Society Home, *c.* 1912.

THE ABBEY SCHOOL for young ladies in Malvern Wells probably dates from the 1870's. This view of the main building from the rear dates from the 1920's, when it was run by Miss Judson.

THE KITCHEN of the Abbey School c. 1920's.

THE ABBEY SCHOOL obviously expected their young ladies to work in the gardens, as this view shows.

STAFF AND DOMESTICS of the Abbey School c.1920's.

THE RUBY, WELLS ROAD. From about 1900–1906 this late eighteenth-century house was used for apartments. From 1915 it was the home of Henry James Cuff of J.H. Cuff & Co., Mineral Water Manufacturers.

THE ESSINGTON HOTEL from the Wells Road in 1904. At this time the owner was R. Logan.

THE MIDLAND STATION, Malvern Wells, one of two stations in this part of Malvern – the other being for the Great Western. Sadly Malvern Wells no longer has a station.

THE MANSE Malvern Wells, *c.* 1916. Prior to 1914 it was used as a ladies' school. It is now flats.

GOLF COURSE AND LINKS, Malvern Wells, in 1915. Built in 1884, the golf club moved from Longridge Road (off Peachfield) in the 1920's. The house is now split into two.

TANNACHIE COURT, Malvern Wells, in 1927. This is in Lower (now Hanley) Road, and is now the Sherborne Tower Nursing Home.

THE PRIORY, Little Malvern, around 1915. Next to St. Wulstan's Catholic Church, it is now known as Kirklands.

XMAS PARTY BLUES. "This is Donald as he was in the play at the school (Little Malvern) Xmas party". c. 1920's.

ST. RICHARD'S SCHOOL, Little Malvern. A classroom.

THE GYMNASIUM of St. Richard's School.

Five

The Hills

THE KETTLE SINGS. An advertising card for the cafe on Jubilee Drive.

ST. ANN'S WELL around 1870. At this time Thomas Bennett, the photographer, had a studio here, and some of his photographs can be seen in the windows.

A BUSY DAY at St. Ann's Well around the turn of the century.

THE PATH up to St. Ann's Well prior to the First World War.

'BLIND GEORGE' PULLEN played the harmonium at St. Ann's Well virtually every day for over fifty years. Most postcards of St. Ann's Well show him at work. He died in 1936.

WYNDS POINT at British Camp. This was the home of Jenny Lind, the Swedish Nightingale, from 1883 to 1887. This view was taken during the early years of the century.

JENNY LIND, one of the greatest nineteenth-century singers. This photograph was taken *c.* 1880.

THE BRITISH CAMP SWIMMING POOL sometime in the 1930s.

THE ENTRANCE to the British Camp swimming pool.

THE 'WYTCH' PASS, as seen in 1856.

THE WYCHE PASS during the early years of this century.

UPPER AND LOWER WYCHE, *c.* 1910. Now the lower road is access only.

VIEW AT THE WYCHE from near the top of Walwyn Drive about 1908. Some of the houses can still be identified, but nearly everything is now obscured by trees.

THE WYCHE PASS, around 1912.

THE WYCHE END of Jubilee Drive, prior to the First World War. The Wyche Mission Chapel (now Free Church) is on the right. The view is now completely hidden by trees.

THE TOPOSCOPE was installed at the top of the Worcestershire Beacon in 1897 at the time of the Jubliee. At 1,396 ft. above sea level it shows landmarks visible over a very wide area.

THE WORCESTERSHIRE BEACON CAFE, destroyed by fire in 1989, taken some time in the 1950's. Shown here with the Toposcope, the cafe is now unlikely to be replaced.

IVY SCAR ROCK, probably in the 1870's. When this view was taken the hills were still mainly in private hands.

MEET OF THE LEDBURY HOUNDS at British Camp, March 1910.

Six

Around and About

DEER IN EASTNOR PARK during the 1920's. I wonder how long the photographer waited for this shot!

GOODWINS CORNER, Walwyn Road, Colwall, during the early years of the century. The house on the right is Woodstock.

BALLARDS DRIVE, Colwall, is virtually forgotten. The entrance leads off Walwyn Road to Linden Manor. This house still exists but has been extended and much changed.

BALLARDS DRIVE, the Hills, and Jubilee Drive. The cyclists are on what is now Walwyn Road. The road to the left is Camp (now Chase) Road. The Ballards Drive entrance can just be discerned opposite the cyclists.

A COLWALL SCHOOL group in 1924.

THE CENTRE OF COLWALL, with the Colwall Park Hotel on the right and the Colwall Stone on the left, around 1907.

MAIN ROAD, COLWALL, prior to the First World War. The entrance to Brook House is on the right. The cottage beyond the car has disappeared.

THIS COTTAGE still stands at the Ledbury end of Colwall, but the road is much busier than when this was taken before the First World War.

BAZAAR AT NEW COURT, Colwall, July 1908. New Court, on the corner of Church Road, was demolished and replaced in the 1930's.

SAMUEL BRADBURN was a Manure Merchant in Colwall up to about 1916, living at Brockbury Hall.

MARY DUGGAN'S CRICKET TEAM for Cricket Week at Colwall 1958. Mary Duggan is centre front, Betty Snowball extreme right standing, and J.M. Pierce extreme left standing.

THE HORSE & GROOM HOTEL, Colwall, in 1910. The Oddfellows' Hall is on the right. Later renamed the Horse & Jockey, it was recently closed for refurbishment and is now known as the Oddfellows.

A TRAIN PASSING THROUGH COLWALL around 1908.

RIDGWAY CROSS POST OFFICE, 1930. H. Bate was the postmaster at the time. The shop premises are now much changed and are used for residential purposes.

CRADLEY VILLAGE Post Office and shop prior to the First World War.

BOYS' SCHOOL, CRADLEY, *c.* 1909. Next to the church, the building is now used as the Village Hall. A ramp for disabled access has just been installed.

H. HEHIR, grocer and baker of Mathon. He lived at "Badgers" and this photograph was presumably taken during deliveries, probably before the First World War.

STIFFORDS BRIDGE sometime in the 1920's. George F. Lawrence ran the Red Lion Inn on the right, and the Seven Stars Inn is in the distance. This road is now very busy indeed.

CHERRY ORCHARD, GUARLFORD, during the early years of the century. In the foreground is a classical ha-ha. At this time the house was occupied by Christopher Robothan, dairyman.

SEVERN END, HANLEY CASTLE, 1910, the home of Sir Edmund Lechmere, Bt. This view is of the rear.

BLACKMORE GRANGE, HANLEY SWAN, in 1905. Foliage has now obliterated this view.

MADRESFIELD VILLAGE. An almost unchanged view. About two thirds of the building on the right is *c.* sixteenth century, the rest probably Victorian.

MADRESFIELD COURT. One of the entrances to the grounds, shown here prior to 1912.

MADRESFIELD SHOW, AUGUST 1928. Lady Mary and Lady Dorothy Lygon, daughters of the 7th Earl of Beauchamp, and other spectators.

MADRESFIELD POST OFFICE and the Parish Church of St. Mary the Virgin just prior to the First World War. Although no longer a Post Office, the letter box in the wall remains.

AGRICULTURAL SHOW DAY at Madresfield, 1902. Judging the hunters.

UPPER WELLAND VILLAGE during the early part of the century. Although the roof line has changed, the Hawthorn Inn is just recognisable second on the right.

UPPER WELLAND VILLAGE around the time of the First World War. The road on the left is Chase Road and on the right is Watery Lane.

THE REVD CECIL HUGHES (far right) was Curate (1866) and then Vicar of Powick from 1867–1916, a total of over 50 years.

CALLOW END POST OFFICE, formerly Cedar Cottage. When this was taken prior to the First World War, it had only recently become a Post Office and was run by Mrs Cooke.

THE SMITHY, CASTLEMORTON, in 1923. The Robin Hood public house is on the far side.

HUNTER'S COTTAGE, CASTLEMORTON, 1922, was occupied by the Hamblin family.

MEMBERS OF THE HAMBLIN FAMILY outside Hunter's Cottage, 1922.

Seven

People and Places

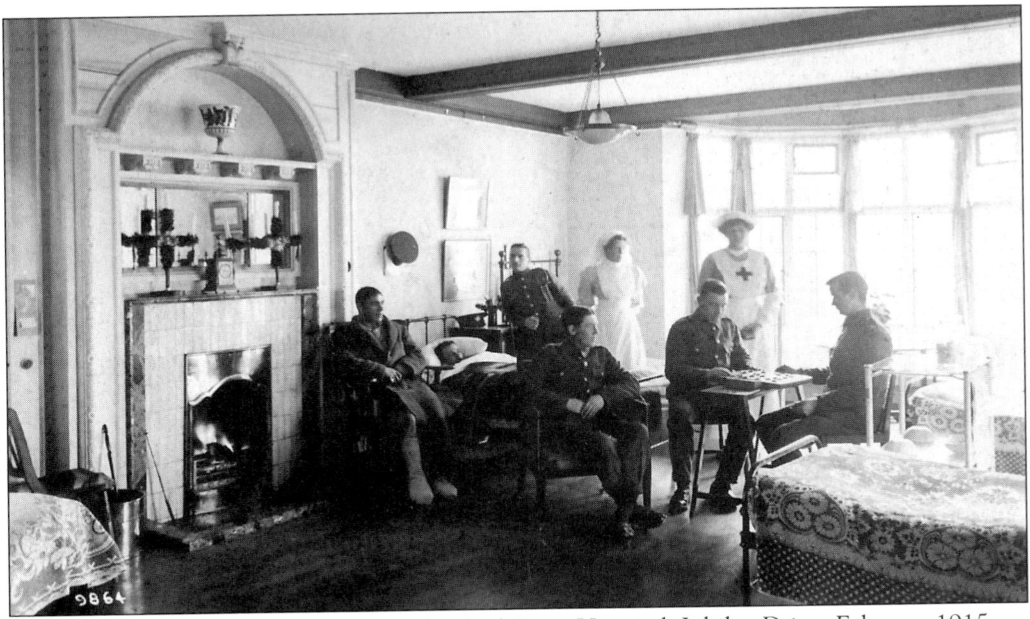

WOUNDED SOLDIERS at Brand Lodge Red Cross Hospital, Jubilee Drive, February 1915.

GEORGE BERNARD SHAW and Roy Limbert at Malvern during a Festival in the late 1930's. Roy Limbert founded, with Sir Barry Jackson, the Malvern Festival in 1929. He was joint director for nine years until, in 1938, he assumed sole control.

CEDRIC HARDWICKE and cast in *Return to Sanity* in the 1937 Malvern Festival.

BILLY GAMMON and his orchestra at the Winter Gardens during the Summer Season, 1936.

OPENING OF THE NEW ART SCHOOL in Albert Road in 1928. This is now Malvern Hills College.

LADY FRANCES BALFOUR, President of the National Council of Women, opening new bungalows for women wage owners, at Pickersleigh Close, Malvern Link, May 1922.

THIS CLEM WALTON PHOTOGRAPH appears to be of a foundation stone laying ceremony – but is it? And where is the site?

:ONSERVATIVE FETE, June 1926, at Fern Lodge, Worcester Road, the home of Mr and Mrs ɅIorgan. Opened by Lady Brooke, the fête concluded in the evening with political speeches!

ANOTHER CONSERVATIVE FETE, this time in July 1928. Again at Fern Lodge, this one was opened by Mrs Stanley Baldwin, wife of the Prime Minister and Worcestershire M.P.

THE LAMPLIGHTER and his assistant (!) in Upper Chase Road, Barnards Green.

FUNERAL OF P.C. HOWARD OVERTON, who was killed on Whit Monday 1928 in an attempt to save a child's life. Overton, of 4 Moorlands Road, was on point duty near the railway bridge at Malvern, when he fell in front of a car when trying to save a $2\frac{1}{2}$-year-old child who ran across the road. The procession is seen here on route from Moorlands Road to Holy Trinity Church. He joined the force in 1903, at the age of 26, and was the first plain clothes officer in Malvern.

FUNERAL OF R.J. CHAPMAN, formerly Chief Inspector at Paddington Station in September 1924. He lived at Maryville, St. Andrews Road.

'BLIND FRED' of Malvern, started delivering newspapers in 1914. This photograph was taken in 1926, when he was said to have walked 111,410 miles on his rounds.

A MALVERN WEDDING. Clem Walton photographed this unidentified wedding group, probably just before the First World War. Can anyone identify the family?

DR JAMES MANBY GULLY (1802–82), the most famous of the water cure doctors. He arrived in Malvern in October 1842 and bought two houses on the Wells Road (later the Tudor Hotel).

SOME OF THE JOYS of the Water Cure.

THE BROTHERS LAYTON born in Upper Howsell between 1839 and 1855. They are shown here, with their respective ages, in 1922.

MALVERN AND TEWKESBURY Junction Signal Box. The line was opened in 1864 and closed in 1952.

C.R. HILL, taken *c.* 1937. He was a local referee and worked for the Gas Board in Malvern.

THE GAS BOARD was in Moorlands Road. This van, driven by C.R. Hill, shows the restrained form of vehicle advertising not uncommon in the 1930's.

THIS MALVERN COLLEGE VAN was driven by C.R. Hill prior to his work for the Gas Board.

THESE FOUR PHOTOGRAPHS were taken pre–1920 by two local photographers at the same event on the same day, but where was it and what was the event?

WHO?

WHAT?

WHERE?

ST. MATTHIAS (TEMPERANCE) GYMNASTIC CLUB. *c.* 1903–06. Apparently taken at their headquarters at the Church Institute. The group included (left to right) back row: no. 1, F. Davis; no. 4, Arthur Wall; no. 5, John Preece. Second row: nos 3 and 4, Albert and William Littlewood. Front row: no.2, Harry Pitt. Preece was, for several years, gymnastic tutor at the Institute, which provided dumb bells, clubs, vaulting horses, horizontal bars, etc.

MALVERN LINK EXCELSIORS football team 1906–07 were based at Pickersleigh Road.

SUN ECLIPSE at Malvern on 30 August 1905 at 12.34 p.m.

THE FODEN DISASTER. On 1 July 1926 this Foden steam lorry loaded with bricks ran out of control on Camp Hill, near British Camp, going off the road and hitting a tree. The driver, Albert Flower of Worcester, was killed by the load of bricks, which slid forward.

TOMATOLAND after the gales, c. 1960's. The firm of tomato growers was in Pickersleigh Road.

DAVID LLOYD GEORGE at the Camp of the 13th Pioneer Battalion of the Glosters at Malvern, 13 June 1915.

AN UNIDENTIFIED MILITARY group from the First World War. Some of the soldiers included are A.N. Rowland, P.J. Jones and M. Joster.

3/8TH WORCESTERS in camp, Malvern, 1915.

SOUTH MIDLANDS T.A., R.A.M.C. at Malvern during the First World War.

16TH SERVICE R.W.R. in camp at Malvern during the First World War. This view shows D Company's lines decorated for sports.

MUSIC IN CAMP from the 13th Glosters during the First World War.